ANCESTRAL ILLUMINATION

A Guided Journal *for* Black Tarot

....

Written by

NYASHA WILLIAMS

Illustrations by

KIMISHKA NAIDOO

RP **STUDIO**

PHILADELPHIA

RP Studio™
Hachette Book Group
1290 Avenue of the Americas, New York, NY 10104
www.runningpress.com
@Running_Press

Printed in China

First Edition: December 2022

Published by RP Studio, an imprint of Perseus Books, LLC, a subsidiary of Hachette Book Group, Inc. The RP Studio name and logo are trademarks of the Hachette Book Group.

The publisher is not responsible for websites (or their content) that are not owned by the publisher.

Design by Joanna Price

ISBN: 978-0-7624-7970-2

1010

10 9 8 7 6 5 4 3 2 1

This journal belongs to:

....

The Star

Introduction

ONE OF THE BEST WAYS to process, create, or work through things is by getting them down on paper. Whether it is a new book idea, shadow work that I need to address, or tracking experiences and thoughts throughout my spiritual journey, writing it all down is fundamental in allowing me to self-reflect, visualize ideas, and release heavy emotions. I partake in tarot and divination routinely, connecting with my Ancestors and spiritual guides for clarification, wisdom, and confirmation.

I am a transracial adoptee, adopted at two weeks old, who has reconnected with my biological family on my maternal side. This has made searching for my identity a pilgrimage, one in which I have often identified my passions as they've grown. As an African American, I have been disconnected from my Ancestors, and their traditions and spiritual practices, because of the transatlantic slave trade and slavery in America. Being adopted, I have been disconnected from my bloodline and have had to learn family histories through secondary and tertiary sources.

I've discovered some of the missing links to my identity through partaking in divination while recording my growth with the help of various tools. It has been a wholesome experience that has included building relationships, receiving guidance, and obtaining affirmation for my work on Earth by known and unknown Ancestors. My hope is that *Ancestral Illumination* aids in opening doors and pathways for you on your spiritual journey and helps with closing areas you need to release or move past.

May this journal provide comfort on your spiritual walk and encourage brave self-reflection toward your growth and evolution.

Much gratitude,

N. Williams

Engaging *in* Ancestral Work

ANCESTRAL MATHEMATICS

"In order to be born, you needed:

2 parents

4 grandparents

8 great-grandparents

16 second great-grandparents

32 third great-grandparents

64 fourth great-grandparents

128 fifth great-grandparents

256 sixth great-grandparents

512 seventh great-grandparents

1,024 eighth great-grandparents

2,048 ninth great-grandparents

For you to be born today from 12 previous generations,
you needed a total of 4,094 ancestors over the last 400 years.

Think for a moment—How many struggles? How many
battles? How many difficulties? How much sadness? How much
happiness? How many love stories? How many expressions of
hope for the future?—did your ancestors have to undergo
for you to exist in this present moment. . . ."

—Author unknown

WHEN YOU CHOOSE TO CONNECT with your Ancestors, you aren't "connecting" with them; you are *reconnecting* with them. You are your Ancestors. Your walk on Earth involves remembering all of them, realizing they are present within you, and understanding that you are a continuation of them. We have been stripped of this knowledge by capitalism, white supremacy, and colonization's facades and narratives around Indigenous spiritual practices and traditions. These structures harmed our identity; it is shameful for any people to demonize the revering of their Ancestors while blindly worshipping the heroes of others.

A major part of our healing involves realigning with our Ancestors and honoring the truth that we are a part of their masterpieces. They worked hard to assure that you are here and present today. Although pain and trauma travel through ancestral lineage, so too can abundance and healing; in healing ourselves, we heal our bloodlines.

Where to begin? While everyone's path looks different, here are some steps I recommend to help you reconnect with your Ancestors and spiritual guides.

1. **Research and visit spaces connected to your ancestry.**
2. **Speak to your Ancestors.** Let them know you are open to connecting (and why). Say, for example, "Ancestors and Spirit Guides known and unknown, who want the best for me in my family . . ."
3. **Spend time with family and recover stories.** Create albums and documentation of anything you want to pass down the family line.
4. **Build an ancestral altar.** Create a sacred space, and make a regular practice of visiting. Pictures and heirlooms are a great place to start, but, understanding that you might not have any of those items, use objects based on your intuition about what would please them.
5. **Use divination tools.** Remember to clear any tool's energy before use; energetic cleansing can be done by using smoke, the sun, the moon, water, and visualization, to name a few.

And last but surely not least, track all your hard work. Keep journaling.
Happy divining.

Rituals *for* the Moon Phases

RITUALS FOR THE NEW MOON

+ Set goals and intentions.
+ Start new projects and develop new ideas.
+ Manifest (relay your desires, hopes, goals, and dreams to the universe).
+ Cleanse your (mental and physical) space.

RITUALS FOR THE WAXING MOON (Crescent, First Quarter, Gibbous)

+ Plan and prepare (waxing crescent).
+ Take action toward your intentions (first quarter).
+ Fine-tune and reevaluate plans and intentions (waxing gibbous).

RITUALS FOR THE FULL MOON

+ Take a spiritual bath.
+ Cleanse your (mental and physical) space.
+ Charge your spiritual tools.
+ Meditate.
+ Dance.

RITUALS FOR THE WANING MOON (Gibbous, Third Quarter, Crescent)

+ Practice gratitude (waning gibbous).
+ Release anything you have outgrown (third quarter).
+ Reflect and rest after all your hard work (waning crescent).

Questions *to* Meditate On

QUESTIONS TO ASK YOURSELF TO BEGIN THE MONTH

- ✦ What am I stepping into this month?
- ✦ What should I do more of this month?
- ✦ What should I do less of this month?
- ✦ Where do I need more structure in my life?
- ✦ What unhealthy habits do I need to break?

QUESTIONS TO ASK YOURSELF WEEK TWO

- ✦ Where can I find creative inspiration?
- ✦ Where in my life am I invited to liberate more fully?
- ✦ What is trying to come forward in my life?
- ✦ Which venture should I focus my attention on?
- ✦ What will allow me to make the best possible decision?

QUESTIONS TO ASK YOURSELF WEEK THREE

- ✦ What is something I could do right now that would bring me peace?
- ✦ Where is love in my life?
- ✦ How can I add happiness to my life?
- ✦ Where do I need to be kinder to myself?
- ✦ Where do I need to be kinder to others?

QUESTIONS TO ASK YOURSELF WEEK FOUR

+ What should I look out for?
+ What am I ignoring or not seeing?
+ What am I in denial about?
+ Where am I restricting myself?
+ How can I balance my emotions?

QUESTIONS TO ASK YOURSELF LOOKING BACK AT THE MONTH

+ What is something wonderful about the world?
+ What will help me restore my hope in the future?
+ What mistakes do I need to forgive myself for?
+ What is something for which I deserve acknowledgment?
+ Where does my potential lie?

Tarot Reading Example

Name of deck used in reading

DECK USED

Name of chosen spread

SPREAD TITLE

DATE   S M T W T F S   **MOON PHASE**

Chosen tarot prompt

QUESTION   ANSWER IN A READING: ◯ YES ◯ NO ◯ MAYBE

CARD(S) PULLED

Stickers or drawings of the card(s) pulled

CARD(S) MEANING   **SUIT(S)**

Air, fire, water, earth

ELEMENT(S)   **NUMBER(S)**

COLOR(S)   **SYMBOLISM**

INTUITIVE INTERPRETATION *Record your inner wisdom and knowledge after*

reflecting on the pulled card(s).

KEYWORDS AND MESSAGES *Take note of words that come to mind, and add to your*

interpretation of the reading using the tarot cheat sheets and/or tarot guidebook.

STEPS AFTER READING *Take note of what needs to happen next. What wisdom or*

guidance did you receive that you need to put into action?

Moments of Gratitude

———

List three things you are grateful for at this present moment.

Month 1

Tarot Reading

DECK USED

SPREAD TITLE

DATE   S M T W T F S   **MOON PHASE**

QUESTION   ANSWER IN A READING: ◯ YES ◯ NO ◯ MAYBE

CARD(S) PULLED

CARD(S) MEANING

SUIT(S)

ELEMENT(S)

NUMBER(S)

COLOR(S)

SYMBOLISM

INTUITIVE INTERPRETATION

KEYWORDS AND MESSAGES

STEPS AFTER READING

Moments of Gratitude

Tarot Reading

DECK USED

SPREAD TITLE

DATE   S M T W T F S   MOON PHASE

QUESTION   ANSWER IN A READING: ◯ YES ◯ NO ◯ MAYBE

CARD(S) PULLED

CARD(S) MEANING

SUIT(S)

ELEMENT(S)

NUMBER(S)

COLOR(S)

SYMBOLISM

INTUITIVE INTERPRETATION

KEYWORDS AND MESSAGES

STEPS AFTER READING

Moments of Gratitude

Tarot Reading

DECK USED

SPREAD TITLE

DATE   S M T W T F S   MOON PHASE

QUESTION   ANSWER IN A READING: ◯ YES ◯ NO ◯ MAYBE

CARD(S) PULLED

CARD(S) MEANING

SUIT(S)

ELEMENT(S)

NUMBER(S)

COLOR(S)

SYMBOLISM

INTUITIVE INTERPRETATION

KEYWORDS AND MESSAGES

STEPS AFTER READING

Moments of Gratitude

Tarot Reading

DECK USED

SPREAD TITLE

DATE   S M T W T F S   **MOON PHASE**

QUESTION   ANSWER IN A READING: ◯ YES ◯ NO ◯ MAYBE

CARD(S) PULLED

CARD(S) MEANING

SUIT(S)

ELEMENT(S)

NUMBER(S)

COLOR(S)

SYMBOLISM

INTUITIVE INTERPRETATION

KEYWORDS AND MESSAGES

STEPS AFTER READING

Moments of Gratitude

Monthly Tarot Reading Reflection

DATE

MOON PHASE

MOST COMMON CARDS PULLED

RECURRING NUMBERS, IMAGERY, AND SYMBOLISM

MOST COMMON SUITS _____

_____

MAJOR ARCANA THEMES _____

_____

FAMILY COURT CARD THEMES _____

_____

_____

MINOR ARCANA THEMES _____

_____

_____

INTROSPECTION _____

_____

_____

ACTION STEPS _____

_____

_____

Month 2

Tarot Reading

DECK USED

SPREAD TITLE

DATE   S M T W T F S   MOON PHASE

QUESTION   ANSWER IN A READING: ◯ YES ◯ NO ◯ MAYBE

CARD(S) PULLED

CARD(S) MEANING

SUIT(S)

ELEMENT(S)

NUMBER(S)

COLOR(S)

SYMBOLISM

INTUITIVE INTERPRETATION

KEYWORDS AND MESSAGES

STEPS AFTER READING

Moments of Gratitude

Tarot Reading

DECK USED

SPREAD TITLE

DATE   S M T W T F S   **MOON PHASE**

QUESTION   ANSWER IN A READING: ◯ YES ◯ NO ◯ MAYBE

CARD(S) PULLED

CARD(S) MEANING

SUIT(S)

ELEMENT(S)

NUMBER(S)

COLOR(S)

SYMBOLISM

INTUITIVE INTERPRETATION _____

KEYWORDS AND MESSAGES _____

STEPS AFTER READING _____

Moments of Gratitude

Tarot Reading

DECK USED

SPREAD TITLE

DATE   S M T W T F S   **MOON PHASE**

QUESTION   ANSWER IN A READING: ◯ YES ◯ NO ◯ MAYBE

CARD(S) PULLED

CARD(S) MEANING

SUIT(S)

ELEMENT(S)

NUMBER(S)

COLOR(S)

SYMBOLISM

INTUITIVE INTERPRETATION

KEYWORDS AND MESSAGES

STEPS AFTER READING

Moments of Gratitude

Tarot Reading

DECK USED

SPREAD TITLE

DATE   S M T W T F S   **MOON PHASE**

QUESTION   ANSWER IN A READING: ◯ YES ◯ NO ◯ MAYBE

CARD(S) PULLED

CARD(S) MEANING

SUIT(S)

ELEMENT(S)

NUMBER(S)

COLOR(S)

SYMBOLISM

INTUITIVE INTERPRETATION

KEYWORDS AND MESSAGES

STEPS AFTER READING

Moments of Gratitude

Monthly Tarot Reading Reflection

DATE

MOON PHASE

MOST COMMON CARDS PULLED

RECURRING NUMBERS, IMAGERY, AND SYMBOLISM

MOST COMMON SUITS _____

_____

MAJOR ARCANA THEMES _____

_____

FAMILY COURT CARD THEMES _____

_____

_____

MINOR ARCANA THEMES _____

_____

_____

INTROSPECTION _____

_____

_____

ACTION STEPS _____

_____

_____

Month 3

Tarot Reading

DECK USED

SPREAD TITLE

DATE   S M T W T F S   **MOON PHASE**

QUESTION   ANSWER IN A READING: ◯ YES ◯ NO ◯ MAYBE

CARD(S) PULLED

CARD(S) MEANING _____

SUIT(S) _____

ELEMENT(S) _____

NUMBER(S) _____

COLOR(S) _____

SYMBOLISM _____

INTUITIVE INTERPRETATION _____

_____

KEYWORDS AND MESSAGES _____

_____

STEPS AFTER READING _____

_____

Moments of Gratitude

Tarot Reading

DECK USED

SPREAD TITLE

DATE   S M T W T F S   **MOON PHASE**

QUESTION   **ANSWER IN A READING:** ◯ YES ◯ NO ◯ MAYBE

> **CARD(S) PULLED**

CARD(S) MEANING

SUIT(S)

ELEMENT(S)

NUMBER(S)

COLOR(S)

SYMBOLISM

INTUITIVE INTERPRETATION

KEYWORDS AND MESSAGES

STEPS AFTER READING

Moments of Gratitude

Tarot Reading

DECK USED

SPREAD TITLE

DATE   S M T W T F S   **MOON PHASE**

QUESTION   ANSWER IN A READING: ◯ YES ◯ NO ◯ MAYBE

CARD(S) PULLED

CARD(S) MEANING

SUIT(S)

ELEMENT(S)

NUMBER(S)

COLOR(S)

SYMBOLISM

INTUITIVE INTERPRETATION

KEYWORDS AND MESSAGES

STEPS AFTER READING

Moments of Gratitude

Tarot Reading

DECK USED

SPREAD TITLE

DATE   S M T W T F S   **MOON PHASE**

QUESTION   ANSWER IN A READING: ◯ YES ◯ NO ◯ MAYBE

CARD(S) PULLED

CARD(S) MEANING _____

SUIT(S) _____

ELEMENT(S) _____

NUMBER(S) _____

COLOR(S) _____

SYMBOLISM _____

INTUITIVE INTERPRETATION _____

_____

KEYWORDS AND MESSAGES _____

_____

STEPS AFTER READING _____

_____

Moments of Gratitude

Monthly Tarot Reading Reflection

DATE

MOON PHASE

MOST COMMON CARDS PULLED

RECURRING NUMBERS, IMAGERY, AND SYMBOLISM

MOST COMMON SUITS _____

_____

MAJOR ARCANA THEMES _____

_____

FAMILY COURT CARD THEMES _____

_____

_____

MINOR ARCANA THEMES _____

_____

_____

INTROSPECTION _____

_____

_____

ACTION STEPS _____

_____

_____

Month 4

Tarot Reading

DECK USED

SPREAD TITLE

DATE   S M T W T F S   **MOON PHASE**

QUESTION   ANSWER IN A READING: ◯ YES ◯ NO ◯ MAYBE

CARD(S) PULLED

CARD(S) MEANING

SUIT(S)

ELEMENT(S)

NUMBER(S)

COLOR(S)

SYMBOLISM

INTUITIVE INTERPRETATION _____

KEYWORDS AND MESSAGES _____

STEPS AFTER READING _____

Moments of Gratitude

Tarot Reading

DECK USED

SPREAD TITLE

DATE   S M T W T F S   **MOON PHASE**

QUESTION   **ANSWER IN A READING:** ◯ YES ◯ NO ◯ MAYBE

CARD(S) PULLED

CARD(S) MEANING

SUIT(S)

ELEMENT(S)

NUMBER(S)

COLOR(S)

SYMBOLISM

INTUITIVE INTERPRETATION

KEYWORDS AND MESSAGES

STEPS AFTER READING

Moments of Gratitude

Tarot Reading

___

DECK USED

SPREAD TITLE

DATE   S M T W T F S   **MOON PHASE**

QUESTION   ANSWER IN A READING: ○ YES ○ NO ○ MAYBE

CARD(S) PULLED

CARD(S) MEANING

SUIT(S)

ELEMENT(S)

NUMBER(S)

COLOR(S)

SYMBOLISM

INTUITIVE INTERPRETATION

KEYWORDS AND MESSAGES

STEPS AFTER READING

Moments of Gratitude

Tarot Reading

DECK USED

SPREAD TITLE

DATE   S M T W T F S   MOON PHASE

QUESTION   ANSWER IN A READING: ◯ YES ◯ NO ◯ MAYBE

CARD(S) PULLED

CARD(S) MEANING

SUIT(S)

ELEMENT(S)

NUMBER(S)

COLOR(S)

SYMBOLISM

INTUITIVE INTERPRETATION

KEYWORDS AND MESSAGES

STEPS AFTER READING

Moments of Gratitude

Monthly Tarot Reading Reflection

___

DATE

MOON PHASE

MOST COMMON CARDS PULLED

RECURRING NUMBERS, IMAGERY, AND SYMBOLISM

MOST COMMON SUITS _____

_____

MAJOR ARCANA THEMES _____

_____

FAMILY COURT CARD THEMES _____

_____

_____

MINOR ARCANA THEMES _____

_____

_____

INTROSPECTION _____

_____

_____

ACTION STEPS _____

_____

_____

Month 5

Tarot Reading

DECK USED

_____

SPREAD TITLE

_____

DATE   S M T W T F S   MOON PHASE

_____

QUESTION   ANSWER IN A READING: ◯ YES ◯ NO ◯ MAYBE

CARD(S) PULLED

CARD(S) MEANING

SUIT(S)

ELEMENT(S)

NUMBER(S)

COLOR(S)

SYMBOLISM

INTUITIVE INTERPRETATION

KEYWORDS AND MESSAGES

STEPS AFTER READING

Moments of Gratitude

Tarot Reading

DECK USED

SPREAD TITLE

DATE   S M T W T F S   MOON PHASE

QUESTION   ANSWER IN A READING: ◯ YES ◯ NO ◯ MAYBE

CARD(S) PULLED

CARD(S) MEANING _____

SUIT(S) _____

ELEMENT(S) _____

NUMBER(S) _____

COLOR(S) _____

SYMBOLISM _____

INTUITIVE INTERPRETATION _____

_____

KEYWORDS AND MESSAGES _____

_____

STEPS AFTER READING _____

_____

Moments of Gratitude

Tarot Reading

DECK USED

SPREAD TITLE

DATE   S M T W T F S   **MOON PHASE**

QUESTION   ANSWER IN A READING: ◯ YES ◯ NO ◯ MAYBE

CARD(S) PULLED

CARD(S) MEANING

SUIT(S)

ELEMENT(S)

NUMBER(S)

COLOR(S)

SYMBOLISM

INTUITIVE INTERPRETATION

KEYWORDS AND MESSAGES

STEPS AFTER READING

Moments of Gratitude

Tarot Reading

DECK USED

SPREAD TITLE

DATE   S M T W T F S   **MOON PHASE**

QUESTION   **ANSWER IN A READING:** ◯ YES ◯ NO ◯ MAYBE

CARD(S) PULLED

CARD(S) MEANING

SUIT(S)

ELEMENT(S)

NUMBER(S)

COLOR(S)

SYMBOLISM

INTUITIVE INTERPRETATION

KEYWORDS AND MESSAGES

STEPS AFTER READING

Moments of Gratitude

Monthly Tarot Reading Reflection

DATE

MOON PHASE

MOST COMMON CARDS PULLED

RECURRING NUMBERS, IMAGERY, AND SYMBOLISM

MOST COMMON SUITS _____

_____

MAJOR ARCANA THEMES _____

_____

FAMILY COURT CARD THEMES _____

_____

_____

MINOR ARCANA THEMES _____

_____

_____

INTROSPECTION _____

_____

_____

ACTION STEPS _____

_____

_____

Month 6

Tarot Reading

DECK USED

SPREAD TITLE

DATE   S M T W T F S   **MOON PHASE**

QUESTION   **ANSWER IN A READING:** ◯ YES ◯ NO ◯ MAYBE

CARD(S) PULLED

CARD(S) MEANING

SUIT(S)

ELEMENT(S)

NUMBER(S)

COLOR(S)

SYMBOLISM

INTUITIVE INTERPRETATION

KEYWORDS AND MESSAGES

STEPS AFTER READING

Moments of Gratitude

Tarot Reading

DECK USED

SPREAD TITLE

DATE   S M T W T F S   **MOON PHASE**

QUESTION   ANSWER IN A READING: ◯ YES ◯ NO ◯ MAYBE

CARD(S) PULLED

CARD(S) MEANING

SUIT(S)

ELEMENT(S)

NUMBER(S)

COLOR(S)

SYMBOLISM

INTUITIVE INTERPRETATION _____

KEYWORDS AND MESSAGES _____

STEPS AFTER READING _____

Moments of Gratitude

Tarot Reading

DECK USED

SPREAD TITLE

DATE   S M T W T F S   **MOON PHASE**

QUESTION   ANSWER IN A READING: ◯ YES ◯ NO ◯ MAYBE

CARD(S) PULLED

CARD(S) MEANING

SUIT(S)

ELEMENT(S)

NUMBER(S)

COLOR(S)

SYMBOLISM

INTUITIVE INTERPRETATION

KEYWORDS AND MESSAGES

STEPS AFTER READING

Moments of Gratitude

Tarot Reading

DECK USED

SPREAD TITLE

DATE   S M T W T F S   MOON PHASE

QUESTION   ANSWER IN A READING: ◯ YES ◯ NO ◯ MAYBE

CARD(S) PULLED

CARD(S) MEANING

SUIT(S)

ELEMENT(S)

NUMBER(S)

COLOR(S)

SYMBOLISM

INTUITIVE INTERPRETATION

KEYWORDS AND MESSAGES

STEPS AFTER READING

Moments of Gratitude

Monthly Tarot Reading Reflection

DATE

MOON PHASE

MOST COMMON CARDS PULLED

RECURRING NUMBERS, IMAGERY, AND SYMBOLISM

MOST COMMON SUITS _____

_____

MAJOR ARCANA THEMES _____

_____

FAMILY COURT CARD THEMES _____

_____

_____

MINOR ARCANA THEMES _____

_____

_____

INTROSPECTION _____

_____

_____

ACTION STEPS _____

_____

_____

Month 7

Tarot Reading

DECK USED

SPREAD TITLE

DATE   S M T W T F S   MOON PHASE

QUESTION   ANSWER IN A READING: ◯ YES ◯ NO ◯ MAYBE

CARD(S) PULLED

CARD(S) MEANING

SUIT(S)

ELEMENT(S)

NUMBER(S)

COLOR(S)

SYMBOLISM

INTUITIVE INTERPRETATION

KEYWORDS AND MESSAGES

STEPS AFTER READING

Moments of Gratitude

Tarot Reading

DECK USED

SPREAD TITLE

DATE   S M T W T F S   **MOON PHASE**

QUESTION   **ANSWER IN A READING:** ◯ YES ◯ NO ◯ MAYBE

CARD(S) PULLED

CARD(S) MEANING

SUIT(S)

ELEMENT(S)

NUMBER(S)

COLOR(S)

SYMBOLISM

INTUITIVE INTERPRETATION

KEYWORDS AND MESSAGES

STEPS AFTER READING

Moments of Gratitude

Tarot Reading

DECK USED

SPREAD TITLE

DATE   S M T W T F S   MOON PHASE

QUESTION   ANSWER IN A READING: ◯ YES ◯ NO ◯ MAYBE

CARD(S) PULLED

CARD(S) MEANING

SUIT(S)

ELEMENT(S)

NUMBER(S)

COLOR(S)

SYMBOLISM

INTUITIVE INTERPRETATION

KEYWORDS AND MESSAGES

STEPS AFTER READING

Moments of Gratitude

Tarot Reading

DECK USED

SPREAD TITLE

DATE   S M T W T F S   **MOON PHASE**

QUESTION   ANSWER IN A READING: ◯ YES ◯ NO ◯ MAYBE

> **CARD(S) PULLED**

CARD(S) MEANING

SUIT(S)

ELEMENT(S)

NUMBER(S)

COLOR(S)

SYMBOLISM

INTUITIVE INTERPRETATION

KEYWORDS AND MESSAGES

STEPS AFTER READING

Moments of Gratitude

Monthly Tarot Reading Reflection

DATE

MOON PHASE

MOST COMMON CARDS PULLED

RECURRING NUMBERS, IMAGERY, AND SYMBOLISM

MOST COMMON SUITS _____

_____

MAJOR ARCANA THEMES _____

_____

FAMILY COURT CARD THEMES _____

_____

_____

MINOR ARCANA THEMES _____

_____

_____

INTROSPECTION _____

_____

_____

ACTION STEPS _____

_____

_____

Month 8

Tarot Reading

DECK USED

SPREAD TITLE

DATE   S M T W T F S   MOON PHASE

QUESTION   ANSWER IN A READING: ◯ YES ◯ NO ◯ MAYBE

CARD(S) PULLED

CARD(S) MEANING

SUIT(S)

ELEMENT(S)

NUMBER(S)

COLOR(S)

SYMBOLISM

INTUITIVE INTERPRETATION

KEYWORDS AND MESSAGES

STEPS AFTER READING

Moments of Gratitude

Tarot Reading

DECK USED

SPREAD TITLE

DATE   S M T W T F S   **MOON PHASE**

QUESTION   **ANSWER IN A READING:** ◯ YES ◯ NO ◯ MAYBE

CARD(S) PULLED

CARD(S) MEANING

SUIT(S)

ELEMENT(S)

NUMBER(S)

COLOR(S)

SYMBOLISM

INTUITIVE INTERPRETATION

KEYWORDS AND MESSAGES

STEPS AFTER READING

Moments of Gratitude

Tarot Reading

DECK USED

SPREAD TITLE

DATE   S M T W T F S   **MOON PHASE**

QUESTION   ANSWER IN A READING: ◯ YES ◯ NO ◯ MAYBE

CARD(S) PULLED

CARD(S) MEANING

SUIT(S)

ELEMENT(S)

NUMBER(S)

COLOR(S)

SYMBOLISM

INTUITIVE INTERPRETATION

KEYWORDS AND MESSAGES

STEPS AFTER READING

Moments of Gratitude

Tarot Reading

DECK USED

SPREAD TITLE

DATE   S M T W T F S   MOON PHASE

QUESTION   ANSWER IN A READING: ◯ YES ◯ NO ◯ MAYBE

CARD(S) PULLED

CARD(S) MEANING

SUIT(S)

ELEMENT(S)

NUMBER(S)

COLOR(S)

SYMBOLISM

INTUITIVE INTERPRETATION

KEYWORDS AND MESSAGES

STEPS AFTER READING

Moments of Gratitude

Monthly Tarot Reading Reflection

DATE

MOON PHASE

MOST COMMON CARDS PULLED

RECURRING NUMBERS, IMAGERY, AND SYMBOLISM

MOST COMMON SUITS _____

_____

MAJOR ARCANA THEMES _____

_____

FAMILY COURT CARD THEMES _____

_____

_____

MINOR ARCANA THEMES _____

_____

_____

INTROSPECTION _____

_____

_____

ACTION STEPS _____

_____

_____

Month 9

Tarot Reading

DECK USED

SPREAD TITLE

DATE   S M T W T F S

MOON PHASE

QUESTION   ANSWER IN A READING: ◯ YES ◯ NO ◯ MAYBE

CARD(S) PULLED

CARD(S) MEANING

SUIT(S)

ELEMENT(S)

NUMBER(S)

COLOR(S)

SYMBOLISM

INTUITIVE INTERPRETATION

KEYWORDS AND MESSAGES

STEPS AFTER READING

Moments of Gratitude

Tarot Reading

DECK USED

SPREAD TITLE

DATE   S M T W T F S   MOON PHASE

QUESTION   ANSWER IN A READING: ◯ YES ◯ NO ◯ MAYBE

CARD(S) PULLED

CARD(S) MEANING

SUIT(S)

ELEMENT(S)

NUMBER(S)

COLOR(S)

SYMBOLISM

INTUITIVE INTERPRETATION

KEYWORDS AND MESSAGES

STEPS AFTER READING

Moments of Gratitude

Tarot Reading

DECK USED

SPREAD TITLE

DATE　　　S M T W T F S　　**MOON PHASE**

QUESTION　　　ANSWER IN A READING: ◯ YES ◯ NO ◯ MAYBE

CARD(S) PULLED

CARD(S) MEANING

SUIT(S)

ELEMENT(S)

NUMBER(S)

COLOR(S)

SYMBOLISM

INTUITIVE INTERPRETATION

KEYWORDS AND MESSAGES

STEPS AFTER READING

Moments of Gratitude

Tarot Reading

DECK USED

SPREAD TITLE

DATE

S M T W T F S

MOON PHASE

QUESTION

ANSWER IN A READING: ◯ YES ◯ NO ◯ MAYBE

CARD(S) PULLED

CARD(S) MEANING

SUIT(S)

ELEMENT(S)

NUMBER(S)

COLOR(S)

SYMBOLISM

INTUITIVE INTERPRETATION

KEYWORDS AND MESSAGES

STEPS AFTER READING

Moments of Gratitude

Monthly Tarot Reading Reflection

DATE

MOON PHASE

MOST COMMON CARDS PULLED

RECURRING NUMBERS, IMAGERY, AND SYMBOLISM

MOST COMMON SUITS _____

_____

MAJOR ARCANA THEMES _____

_____

FAMILY COURT CARD THEMES _____

_____

_____

MINOR ARCANA THEMES _____

_____

_____

INTROSPECTION _____

_____

_____

ACTION STEPS _____

_____

_____

Month 10

Tarot Reading

DECK USED

SPREAD TITLE

DATE   S M T W T F S   **MOON PHASE**

QUESTION   ANSWER IN A READING: ◯ YES ◯ NO ◯ MAYBE

CARD(S) PULLED

CARD(S) MEANING

SUIT(S)

ELEMENT(S)

NUMBER(S)

COLOR(S)

SYMBOLISM

INTUITIVE INTERPRETATION

KEYWORDS AND MESSAGES

STEPS AFTER READING

Moments of Gratitude

Tarot Reading

DECK USED

SPREAD TITLE

DATE   S M T W T F S   MOON PHASE

QUESTION   ANSWER IN A READING: ◯ YES ◯ NO ◯ MAYBE

CARD(S) PULLED

CARD(S) MEANING

SUIT(S)

ELEMENT(S)

NUMBER(S)

COLOR(S)

SYMBOLISM

INTUITIVE INTERPRETATION

KEYWORDS AND MESSAGES

STEPS AFTER READING

Moments of Gratitude

Tarot Reading

DECK USED

SPREAD TITLE

DATE   S M T W T F S   **MOON PHASE**

QUESTION   ANSWER IN A READING: ◯ YES ◯ NO ◯ MAYBE

CARD(S) PULLED

CARD(S) MEANING

SUIT(S)

ELEMENT(S)

NUMBER(S)

COLOR(S)

SYMBOLISM

INTUITIVE INTERPRETATION

KEYWORDS AND MESSAGES

STEPS AFTER READING

Moments of Gratitude

Tarot Reading

DECK USED

SPREAD TITLE

DATE   S M T W T F S   **MOON PHASE**

QUESTION   ANSWER IN A READING: ◯ YES ◯ NO ◯ MAYBE

CARD(S) PULLED

CARD(S) MEANING

SUIT(S)

ELEMENT(S)

NUMBER(S)

COLOR(S)

SYMBOLISM

INTUITIVE INTERPRETATION

KEYWORDS AND MESSAGES

STEPS AFTER READING

Moments of Gratitude

Monthly Tarot Reading Reflection

———

DATE

MOON PHASE

MOST COMMON CARDS PULLED

RECURRING NUMBERS, IMAGERY, AND SYMBOLISM

MOST COMMON SUITS _____

_____

MAJOR ARCANA THEMES _____

_____

FAMILY COURT CARD THEMES _____

_____

_____

MINOR ARCANA THEMES _____

_____

_____

INTROSPECTION _____

_____

_____

ACTION STEPS _____

_____

_____

Month 11

Tarot Reading

DECK USED

SPREAD TITLE

DATE   S M T W T F S   **MOON PHASE**

QUESTION   ANSWER IN A READING: ◯ YES ◯ NO ◯ MAYBE

CARD(S) PULLED

CARD(S) MEANING

SUIT(S)

ELEMENT(S)

NUMBER(S)

COLOR(S)

SYMBOLISM

INTUITIVE INTERPRETATION

KEYWORDS AND MESSAGES

STEPS AFTER READING

Moments of Gratitude

Tarot Reading

DECK USED

SPREAD TITLE

DATE   S M T W T F S   **MOON PHASE**

QUESTION   ANSWER IN A READING: ⬭ YES ⬭ NO ⬭ MAYBE

CARD(S) PULLED

CARD(S) MEANING

SUIT(S)

ELEMENT(S)

NUMBER(S)

COLOR(S)

SYMBOLISM

INTUITIVE INTERPRETATION

KEYWORDS AND MESSAGES

STEPS AFTER READING

Moments of Gratitude

Tarot Reading

DECK USED

SPREAD TITLE

DATE S M T W T F S **MOON PHASE**

QUESTION ANSWER IN A READING: ◯ YES ◯ NO ◯ MAYBE

CARD(S) PULLED

CARD(S) MEANING

SUIT(S)

ELEMENT(S)

NUMBER(S)

COLOR(S)

SYMBOLISM

INTUITIVE INTERPRETATION

KEYWORDS AND MESSAGES

STEPS AFTER READING

Moments of Gratitude

Tarot Reading

DECK USED

SPREAD TITLE

DATE   S M T W T F S   **MOON PHASE**

QUESTION   ANSWER IN A READING: ◯ YES ◯ NO ◯ MAYBE

CARD(S) PULLED

CARD(S) MEANING

SUIT(S)

ELEMENT(S)

NUMBER(S)

COLOR(S)

SYMBOLISM

INTUITIVE INTERPRETATION

KEYWORDS AND MESSAGES

STEPS AFTER READING

Moments of Gratitude

Monthly Tarot Reading Reflection

_____

DATE   MOON PHASE

....
                    MOST COMMON CARDS PULLED

....

....
          RECURRING NUMBERS, IMAGERY, AND SYMBOLISM

....

MOST COMMON SUITS _____

_____

MAJOR ARCANA THEMES _____

_____

FAMILY COURT CARD THEMES _____

_____

_____

MINOR ARCANA THEMES _____

_____

_____

INTROSPECTION _____

_____

_____

ACTION STEPS _____

_____

_____

Month 12

Tarot Reading

DECK USED

SPREAD TITLE

DATE   S M T W T F S   **MOON PHASE**

QUESTION   **ANSWER IN A READING:** ◯ YES ◯ NO ◯ MAYBE

CARD(S) PULLED

CARD(S) MEANING

SUIT(S)

ELEMENT(S)

NUMBER(S)

COLOR(S)

SYMBOLISM

INTUITIVE INTERPRETATION

KEYWORDS AND MESSAGES

STEPS AFTER READING

Moments of Gratitude

Tarot Reading

DECK USED

SPREAD TITLE

DATE   S M T W T F S   **MOON PHASE**

QUESTION   ANSWER IN A READING: ◯ YES ◯ NO ◯ MAYBE

CARD(S) PULLED

CARD(S) MEANING

SUIT(S)

ELEMENT(S)

NUMBER(S)

COLOR(S)

SYMBOLISM

INTUITIVE INTERPRETATION

KEYWORDS AND MESSAGES

STEPS AFTER READING

Moments of Gratitude

Tarot Reading

DECK USED

SPREAD TITLE

DATE   S M T W T F S   MOON PHASE

QUESTION   ANSWER IN A READING: ◯ YES ◯ NO ◯ MAYBE

CARD(S) PULLED

CARD(S) MEANING

SUIT(S)

ELEMENT(S)

NUMBER(S)

COLOR(S)

SYMBOLISM

INTUITIVE INTERPRETATION

KEYWORDS AND MESSAGES

STEPS AFTER READING

Moments of Gratitude

Tarot Reading

DECK USED

SPREAD TITLE

DATE   S M T W T F S   MOON PHASE

QUESTION   ANSWER IN A READING: ◯ YES ◯ NO ◯ MAYBE

CARD(S) PULLED

CARD(S) MEANING

SUIT(S)

ELEMENT(S)

NUMBER(S)

COLOR(S)

SYMBOLISM

INTUITIVE INTERPRETATION

KEYWORDS AND MESSAGES

STEPS AFTER READING

Moments of Gratitude

Monthly Tarot Reading Reflection

DATE

MOON PHASE

MOST COMMON CARDS PULLED

RECURRING NUMBERS, IMAGERY, AND SYMBOLISM

MOST COMMON SUITS _____

_____

MAJOR ARCANA THEMES _____

_____

FAMILY COURT CARD THEMES _____

_____

_____

MINOR ARCANA THEMES _____

_____

_____

INTROSPECTION _____

_____

_____

ACTION STEPS _____

_____

_____

The Fool

Tarot Keywords

The Fool (0)
Upright: Possibilities
Reversed: Recklessness
Element: Air
Planet: Uranus
Chakra: Crown
Color: White
Crystal: Clear Quartz
Body Parts/Functions: Ankles, Calves, Nervous System, Eyes

The Magician (1)
Upright: Willpower
Reversed: Poor Planning
Element: Air
Planet: Mercury
Chakras: Solar Plexus, Throat
Colors: Blue, Yellow
Crystals: Aquamarine, Citrine
Body Parts/Functions: Hands, Arms, Lungs, Intestine

The High Priestess (2)
Upright: Instinct
Reversed: Self-Doubt
Element: Water
Planet: Moon
Chakras: Third Eye, Sacral
Colors: Indigo, Orange
Crystals: Lapis Lazuli, Moonstone
Body Parts/Functions: Digestive System, Breasts, Uterus, Pancreas

The Empress (3)
Upright: Creation
Reversed: Creative Block
Element: Water
Planet: Venus
Chakras: Heart, Sacral
Colors: Green, Pink, Turquoise
Crystals: Rose Quartz, Emerald
Body Parts/Functions: Neck, Throat, Lips, Cervix

The Emperor (4)
Upright: Ambition
Reversed: Dictator
Element: Fire
Planet: Mars
Chakras: Solar Plexus, Root
Colors: Red, Orange, Yellow
Crystals: Fire Agate, Hematite, Red Jasper, Garnet
Body Parts/Functions: Blood, Bile, Muscle, Head, Brain, Face

The Hierophant (5)

Upright: Tradition
Reversed: Personal Beliefs
Element: Earth
Planet: Venus
Chakras: Throat
Colors: Blue, Green, Brown
Crystals: Sapphire, Jade, Emerald
Body Parts/Functions: Neck, Throat, Ears, Vocal Cords, Tonsils

The Lovers (6)

Upright: Connection
Reversed: Disharmony
Element: Air
Planet: Mercury
Chakra: Heart
Colors: Green, Pink, Yellow, White
Crystals: Rose Quartz, Jade, Malachite
Body Parts/Functions: Arms, Shoulders, Ribs, Lungs, Nervous System

The Chariot (7)

Upright: Movement
Reversed: Opposition
Element: Water
Planet: Moon
Chakra: Solar Plexus
Colors: Yellow, White, Red
Crystals: Citrine, Ruby, Pearl
Body Parts/Functions: Chest, Stomach, Liver, Pancreas, Gallbladder

Strength (8)

Upright: Endurance
Reversed: Low Energy
Element: Fire
Planet: Sun
Chakra: Heart
Colors: Gold, Yellow, Red
Crystals: Ruby, Tiger's Eye
Body Parts/Functions: Heart, Spinal Cord, Back, Spleen

The Hermit (9)

Upright: Solitude
Reversed: Isolation
Element: Earth
Planet: Mercury
Chakra: Third Eye
Colors: Purple, Indigo
Crystals: Carnelian, Amethyst, Peridot
Body Parts/Functions: Abdomen, Reproductive System

Wheel of Fortune (10)

Upright: Destiny
Reversed: Stagnant
Elements: Fire, Water
Planet: Jupiter

Chakra: Throat
Colors: Blue, Orange, Yellow, Brown, Gold
Crystals: Sapphire, Amethyst, Topaz
Body Parts/Functions: Feet, Hips

Justice (11)

Upright: Balance
Reversed: Unfairness
Element: Air
Planet: Venus
Chakra: Heart
Colors: Green, Copper
Crystals: Emerald, Green Tourmaline, Opal
Body Parts/Functions: Kidneys, Genitals

The Hanged Man (12)

Upright: Surrender
Reversed: Delays
Element: Water
Planet: Neptune
Chakra: Crown
Colors: White, Violet, Blue, Silver
Crystals: Amethyst, Coral, Aquamarine
Body Parts/Functions: Sleep, Hydration

Death (13)

Upright: Metamorphosis

Reversed: Resistance
Element: Water
Planet: Pluto
Chakra: Third Eye
Colors: Brown, Black, Grey, Purple
Crystals: Tiger's Eye, Garnet, Diamond
Body Parts/Functions: Sex Drive, Reproductive System, Blood

Temperance (14)

Upright: Moderation
Reversed: Excess
Element: Fire
Planet: Jupiter
Chakra: Heart
Colors: Red, Crimson, Gold, Indigo
Crystals: Sapphire, Topaz, Diamond
Body Parts/Functions: Liver, Hips, Pelvis, Gallbladder

The Devil (15)

Upright: Bondage
Reversed: Detachment
Element: Earth
Planet: Saturn
Chakra: Root
Colors: Grey, Dark Brown, Black
Crystals: Malachite, Black Onyx, Jet, Obsidian
Body Parts/Functions: Skeleton, Skin, Genitals

The Tower (16)

Upright: Disruption
Reversed: Blocked
Element: Fire
Planet: Mars
Chakras: Root, Solar Plexus
Color: Red
Crystals: Ruby, Garnet, Bloodstone, Red Jasper
Body Parts/Functions: Blood, Muscles, Adrenal Glands

The Star (17)

Upright: Hope
Reversed: Despair
Element: Air
Planet: Uranus
Chakra: Crown
Colors: Blue, Yellow, Purple
Crystals: Onyx, Topaz, Sapphire
Body Parts/Functions: Calves, Ankles, Circulatory System

The Moon (18)

Upright: Delusion
Reversed: Released
Element: Water
Planet/Constellation: Pisces
Chakra: Third Eye
Colors: Purple, Crimson
Crystals: Pearl, Sapphire, Emerald
Body Parts/Functions: Pineal Gland, Lymphatic System, Bodily Fluids, Feet

The Sun (19)

Upright: Success
Reversed: Sadness
Element: Fire
Planet/Star: Sun
Chakra: Solar Plexus
Colors: Yellow, Gold
Crystals: Citrine, Yellow Calcite, Pyrite
Body Parts/Functions: Vitality

Judgment (20)

Upright: Awakening
Reversed: Inner Critic
Element: Fire
Planet: Pluto
Chakra: Crown
Colors: Black, White, Scarlet, Orange
Crystals: Kyanite, Moldavite, Labradorite, Obsidian
Body Parts/Functions: Excretory Systems

The World (21)

Upright: Completion
Reversed: Delay Success
Element: Earth
Planet: Saturn
Chakra: Root

Colors: Black, Grey, Brown
Crystals: Hematite, Black
   Tourmaline, Smoky Quartz
Body Part/Function: Physical Aging

MINOR ARCANA

The Suit of Wands
Fire + Creativity
Aries—Leo—Sagittarius

Ace of Wands
Upright: Inspiration
Reversed: Boredom

Two of Wands
Upright: Contemplation
Reversed: Fear of Change

Three of Wands
Upright: Optimism with a Mission
Reversed: Obstacles

Four of Wands
Upright: Happy Home Life
Reversed: Home Conflicts

Five of Wands
Upright: Conflict
Reversed: Respecting Differences

Six of Wands
Upright: Recognition
Reversed: Excess Pride

Seven of Wands
Upright: Standing Your Ground
Reversed: Giving Up

Eight of Wands
Upright: Quick Developments
Reversed: Slowing Down

Nine of Wands
Upright: Resilience
Reversed: Fatigue

Ten of Wands
Upright: Burden
Reversed: Unwilling to Delegate

Page of Wands (Son)
Upright: Daring
Reversed: Impulsivity

Knight of Wands (Daughter)
Upright: Enthusiasm
Reversed: Lack of Direction

King of Wands (Father)
Upright: Creation
Reversed: Impossible Expectations

Queen of Wands (Mother)
Upright: Vibrancy
Reversed: Insecurity

The Suit of Cups (Baskets)
Water + Emotions
Cancer—Scorpio—Pisces

Ace of Cups
Upright: Emotional Growth
Reversed: Emptiness

Two of Cups
Upright: Love
Reversed: Tension

Three of Cups
Upright: Friendship
Reversed: Overindulgence

Four of Cups
Upright: Apathy
Reversed: Acceptance

Five of Cups
Upright: Loss
Reversed: Finding Peace

Six of Cups
Upright: Inner Child
Reversed: Independence

Seven of Cups
Upright: Searching for Purpose
Reversed: Diversion

Eight of Cups
Upright: Moving On
Reversed: Avoidance

Nine of Cups
Upright: Fulfillment
Reversed: Smugness

Ten of Cups
Upright: Inner Peace
Reversed: Shattered Dreams

Page of Cups (Son)
Upright: Naivete
Reversed: Emotional Immaturity

Knight of Cups (Daughter)
Upright: Romance
Reversed: Fantasy

King of Cups (Father)
Upright: Emotional Self-Control
Reversed: Emotional Manipulation

Queen of Cups (Mother)
Upright: Nurturing
Reversed: Martyrdom

The Suit of Swords (Knives)
Air + Mind
Gemini—Libra—Aquarius

Ace of Swords
Upright: New Focus
Reversed: Chaos

Two of Swords
Upright: Decisions
Reversed: Lesser of Two Evils

Three of Swords
Upright: Pain
Reversed: Recovery

Four of Swords
Upright: Rest
Reversed: Burnout

Five of Swords
Upright: Unbridled Ambition
Reversed: Relief

Six of Swords
Upright: Transition
Reversed: Unresolved Issues

Seven of Swords
Upright: Deception
Reversed: Coming Clean

Eight of Swords
Upright: Isolation
Reversed: New Perspective

Nine of Swords
Upright: Trauma
Reversed: Getting Help

Ten of Swords
Upright: Backstabbing
Reversed: Only Upward

Page of Swords (Son)
Upright: Enthusiasm
Reversed: Manipulation

Knight of Swords (Daughter)
Upright: Passionate
Reversed: Unpredictability

King of Swords (Father)
Upright: Truth
Reversed: Cruel

Queen of Swords (Mother)
Upright: Astute
Reversed: Bitter

The Suit of Pentacles (Coins)
Earth + Material
Taurus—Virgo—Capricorn

Ace of Pentacles
Upright: New Venture
Reversed: Missed Opportunity

Two of Pentacles
Upright: Making Ends Meet
Reversed: Disorganized

Three of Pentacles
Upright: Working in Collaboration
Reversed: Group Conflict

Four of Pentacles
Upright: Budgeting
Reversed: Greediness

Five of Pentacles
Upright: Poverty
Reversed: Recovery

Six of Pentacles
Upright: Giving
Reversed: Strings Attached

Seven of Pentacles
Upright: Investments
Reversed: Work Without Results

Eight of Pentacles
Upright: Discipline
Reversed: Lack of Motivation

Nine of Pentacles
Upright: Refinement
Reversed: Living Beyond Means

Ten of Pentacles
Upright: Satisfaction
Reversed: Fleeting Success

Page of Pentacles (Son)
Upright: Sensuousness
Reversed: Laziness

Knight of Pentacles (Daughter)
Upright: Caution
Reversed: Obsessiveness

King of Pentacles (Father)
Upright: Responsibility
Reversed: Greed

Queen of Pentacles (Mother)
Upright: Creativity and Abundance
Reversed: Smothering

Mother of coins

Tarot Birth Card *in* the Major Arcana

♈ Aries (Ram): March 21–April 19: The Emperor

♉ Taurus (Bull): April 20–May 20: The Hierophant

♊ Gemini (Twins): May 21–June 21: The Lovers

♋ Cancer (Crab): June 22–July 22: The Chariot

♌ Leo (Lion): July 23–August 22: Strength

♍ Virgo (Virgin): August 23–September 22: The Hermit

♎ Libra (Balance): September 23–October 23: Justice

♏ Scorpio (Scorpion): October 24–November 21: Death

♐ Sagittarius (Archer): November 22–December 21: Temperance

♑ Capricorn (Goat): December 22–January 19: The Devil

♒ Aquarius (Water Bearer): January 20–February 18: The Star

♓ Pisces (Fish): February 19–March 20: The Moon

Numerology *in* Divination

One (Ace): Beginnings, Power Unity, Creation

Two: Balance, Duality, Partnership, Choice

Three: Creativity, Outcomes, Self-Expression

Four: Structure, Foundations, Hard Work, Material Achievement

Five: Freedom, Change, Challenge, Uncertainty

Six: Harmony, Love, Integration, Relationships

Seven: Tests, Metaphysics, Contemplation, Spirituality, Withdrawal

Eight: Abundance, Prosperity, Authority, Navigation, Manifestation

Nine: Conclusions, Completion, Achievement, Compassion

Ten: Beginnings and Endings, Infinity, Eternity, Cycles

）●（

)●(

꩜

☽ ● ☾